French Fashion Plates
of the Romantic Era
in Full Color

120 Plates from the
"Petit Courrier des Dames,"
1830–34

Edited by

Judy M. Johnson

DOVER PUBLICATIONS, INC., *New York*

Copyright © 1991 by Dover Publications, Inc.
All rights reserved under Pan American and International Copyright
Conventions.

Published in Canada by General Publishing Company, Ltd., 30 Lesmill Road,
Don Mills, Toronto, Ontario.
Published in the United Kingdom by Constable and Company, Ltd., 3 The
Lanchesters, 162–164 Fulham Palace Road, London W6 9ER.

*French Fashion Plates of the Romantic Era in Full Color: 120 Plates from the "Petit
Courrier des Dames," 1830–34* is a new work, first published by Dover Publications,
Inc., in 1991. It comprises 120 plates from the journal *Petit courrier des dames* (see
Introduction for bibliographic details) along with captions newly translated, and a
new Introduction written, specially for the present edition.
The publisher wishes to thank Mr. Robert C. Kaufmann, Associate Museum
Librarian, Irene Lewisohn Costume Reference Library, The Metropolitan
Museum of Art, for helpful advice and information.

Manufactured in the United States of America
Dover Publications, Inc., 31 East 2nd Street, Mineola, N.Y. 11501

Library of Congress Cataloging-in-Publication Data

French fashion plates of the romantic era in full color : 120 plates from the "Petit
    courrier des dames," 1830–34 / edited by Judy M. Johnson.
        p.   cm.
    ISBN 0-486-26734-2
    1. Costume—France—History—19th century—Pictorial works.
2. Costume—History—19th century—Pictorial works. I. Johnson, Judy M.
II. Petit courrier des dames.
GT871.F74   1991
391′.00944′09034—dc20   90-28122
                                                                              CIP

Introduction

THE SOURCE OF THE PLATES. In the early nineteenth century, Paris consolidated its position as fashion leader of Europe, and the publishing industry responded with a large outpouring of periodicals and fashion plates. The plates were often sold abroad for insertion in local publications. One very successful and influential magazine, the *Petit courrier des dames* (Ladies' Little Messenger), ran from 1821 until 1868, when it was absorbed by the *Journal des demoiselles*. An English-language version published for a while in London was called *Fashion as It Flies; or, the Ladies' Little Messenger of Parisian Fashion*. (The *Petit courrier* color plates in the 1830s included the name and address of the London publishers S. and J. Fuller.)

In the early 1830s, the period covered in the present volume, the *Petit courrier*, subtitled *Journal des modes* (Fashion Journal), appeared every five days. Each octavo issue contained eight pages of text (fashion news, theatrical reviews, stories, poems, historical sketches and the like) and one or two color plates (usually one) on heavier paper.

The plates, numbered continuously, were hand-colored copperplate engravings. Women's clothing was given most attention, each plate generally showing a single outfit in a front view, worn by a standing model, and a back view, with a seated model. The two views are never colored the same way; sometimes, even the engraved patterning is omitted in the back view. There was no description of the plate in the text of the magazine. No artists signed the plates or were otherwise credited in the early 1830s.

Above the illustration on each plate were its serial number and the heading "Modes de Paris" (Paris Fashions). Below the illustration were the name and address of the journal, a reference to the Fullers (see above) and the descriptive caption. In most cases, the name and address of the dressmaker were included in the caption, often with separate credits for milliners, hairdressers, jewelers, florists and other tradesmen; occasionally a separate designer credit was given for a dress. In the present volume, the only text that appears is the captions, translated completely and literally, except that the references to the tradesmen are omitted, as being of interest to specialists only. (The original picture numbers and, in most cases, the dates are added in square brackets at the ends of the captions. A numbering from 1 to 120, pertaining to the present volume only, has been added at caption openings.)

Beginning with May 10, 1833 (illustration 88; page 44, right), the plates bear dates. Dates from July 5, 1831 (illustration 33; page 17, left) through May 5, 1833 (illustration 87; page 44, left) have been supplied from an inspection of complete issues in the New York Public Library. It has not been possible to date the first 32 plates, but to judge from the average number of plates published annually, the present chronological selection begins at the end of 1829 or the beginning of 1830. The plates are reproduced here at a slight enlargement.

FRENCH FASHION IN THE EARLY 1830s. The fashions depicted in the *Petit courrier* are decidedly for the well-to-do and are typical of the Romantic era, when Louis-Philippe was the "citizen king" and the middle class was firmly entrenched. Hugo and Balzac were writing, the French had seized Algiers, and the Gothic Revival was in full swing.

MEN'S CLOTHING. Two articles of dress bequeathed by the French Revolution became standard wear for conservatives: trousers and the top hat. The cut of coats and jackets was modified slightly from time to time in these years, apparently in sympathetic vibration with women's dresses (puffier sleeves, tighter waists), but remained essentially static. Trousers were relatively close-fitting for the full length of the leg. Cravats became simpler. There was still a fair amount of color in men's attire, especially in waistcoats, and the uniformly colored suit was still in the future, but the trend toward the respectability of anonymity was under way.

CHILDREN'S CLOTHING. Little girls dressed like their mothers insofar as possible. Boys up to the age of 12 wore some form of tunic, often skirted, and trousers; after that, they dressed like their fathers.

WOMEN'S CLOTHING. The 1820s had seen a particularly sharp break in women's fashion, when the vertical, sheathed, high-waisted look of the Empire style gave way to a horizontal, wide, full look. By 1830, a woman's body was largely belied by clothing that divided her into three stacked equilateral triangles, the heavily emphasized top two triangles (head and thorax areas) pointing downward, the third (skirt area) pointing upward.

Hairdos were complex, sometimes high-piled, and amplified by jewelry and other ornaments. Hats were large and wide, loaded with flowers, plumes and ribbons. The shoulder line was exaggerated by a variety of augmented collars or diminished capes and sleeveless jackets, not to mention such aids as feather or fur boas. Sleeves were characterized by very large puffed areas (leg-o'-mutton and other styles) now at this point, now at that, along the arm. (Wicker frames or feather cushions were required to maintain the shape.) The waist was as close to its natural position as the many layers of petticoats allowed, but it was pinched to a "wasp" look by very tight corseting. Skirts were stiffened into hollow hemispheres, but were still short enough for the feet to be completely visible. In some dress styles, such as the redingote and the tunic dress, the outer dress (or over-dress) was more or less like a coat that contrasted with the extensively exposed inner dress (under-dress). Décolleté was often a feature, even in daytime wear. (Of course, there were different ensembles for different times of day and different occasions.)

Many types of fabrics were used. The new jacquard looms made a greater variety of weaves widely available, prints were becoming popular and a number of artificial and imitation textiles were on hand. But, above all, a wealthy Parisienne seemed able to lay claim to every fiber in the plant and animal kingdoms (see the textiles mentioned in the captions). Moreover, although the period covered here has been called one in which form predominated over color, a glance through the book will indicate that the clothing was the opposite of drab. Many styles and specific articles of dress were inspired by sixteenth-century models, others by current literature (such as *The Hunchback of Notre-Dame*) or by a faddish interest in exotica (Spain, Islamic lands, India).

GLOSSARY OF MATERIALS AND GARMENTS. Following is an alphabetical listing of items mentioned in the captions. The original French spelling and punctuation are very erratic. Some of the commercial names were highly ephemeral and are virtually impossible to track down. Here and in the captions, some of the French terms have been more or less tentatively equated with fabrics known to have been used in England at the time (the fashion links between the two nations were very close) and cited in C. Willett Cunnington's *English Women's Clothing in the Nineteenth Century*. In such cases, his English-language form is used here, e.g. "mousselaine" instead of the more accurate "mousseline."

Ali Baba:? (a mantle fabric). *Batiste:* Fine fabric, like muslin, usually of cotton, sometimes silk or wool. *Bayadere:* Type of pelerine named for the Hindu dancing girls; in this case, not the (later) fabric of that name. *Beret:* Flat, wide-brimmed hat; not the Basque cap. *Bibi:* Type of bonnet, "English cottage bonnet." *Blonde:* Blonde lace, a silk bobbin lace. *Braganza:?* (a mantle fabric). *Brocade:* material with designs created by weft threads added in place. *Broché:* Velvet or silk with satin figure. *Canezou:* Very short sleeveless jacket like a large collar (see especially illustration 94; page 47, right). *Capote:* Bonnet. *Cashmere:* Twill weave of wool from Himalayan goats (also imitated in Europe with sheep's wool). *Cashmerienne:* A fine woolen material. *Challis:* Thin silk-and-wool textile, often with floral prints. *Chevalière:* A boy's outfit (so called from a resemblance to cavalry uniforms?). *Chiné:* Figured (with threads colored before weaving). *Crepe:* Transparent crimped silk gauze. *Crepe illusion:* A fine, close crepe. *Crepe-lisse:* Uncrimped silk gauze. *Crêpe volant:?* (some type of crepe). *Doña María:?* (term applied to gauze and muslin). *Esmeralda:* White crepe with black and gold embroidery, probably named for the heroine of Hugo's *Hunchback of Notre-Dame* (1831). *Etoffe Chantilly:* Chantilly lace (?). *Ferronnière:* Chain with jewel worn on forehead. *Filet:* Square-mesh lace or net. *Foulard:* Soft, light twilled silk. *Foulard de Smyrne:* "Foulard of Smyrna [city in Turkey]" (no description found). *Gauze:* Transparent porous textile of silk or cotton. *Grand Lama:* Type of mantle. *Gros de Naples:* Corded Italian silk. *Gros des Indes:* Heavy silk with narrow stripes. *Gros d'Orient:?* (apparently a corded or striped fabric). *Jaconet:* Thin cotton textile. *Laine foulard:* Silk-and-wool textile. *Lamé:* Textile with metallic threads. *Mantilla:* Light cape. *Merino:* Thin woolen or silk-and-wool cloth, twilled (from Spanish Merino sheep). *Moire:* Textile with watered appearance. *Mousselaine de laine:* Light woolen cloth like a muslin. *Mousselaine de soie:* Soft silk with mesh like muslin. *Mousselaine Thibet:* Semitransparent silk-and-wool textile. *Muslin:* Semitransparent cotton textile. *Needlepoint lace:* Handmade lace using buttonhole stitches. *Organdy:* Transparent muslin with stiff finish. *Passementerie:* Flat trimming of braid, cord, etc. *Peignoir:* Woman's dressing gown. *Pekin:* Light striped silk. *Pelerine:* Short cape covering shoulders. *Percale:* Fine, slightly glazed calico (cotton cloth). *Pinhead:* Same as pointillé. *Pointillé:* With small drawn, cut or punched points. *Poult de soie:* Rich corded silk. *Redingote:* A man's double-breasted, full-skirted tail coat; a woman's outer dress (like a pelisse-robe) inspired by the cut of the man's coat, often with tucks or puffing. *Ruching:* Plaited or goffered cloth strips. *Satin:* Silk twill glossy on the face and dull at the back. *Satin armure:* Either satin with a self-color design, or perhaps a different satin-weave textile. *Satin à volonté:?* (some kind of satin). *Satin blonde:* Satin flowered in white (as if with blonde lace) on a colored ground. *Satin royal:?* (some kind of satin). *Silk:* Textile from fibers produced by silkworms. *Thibet:* A woolen textile, in this case very likely Mousselaine Thibet (see that entry). *Tissu de l'Inde:* "Textile from India" (is something more specific intended?). *Terry velvet:* Silk with fine cording; or, uncut velvet. *Tulle:* Fine silk net. *Tulle Arachné:* Clear tulle embroidered in light patterns with a mixture of gold and silk (named for the fine weaver who was transformed into a spider in Greek myth). *Tulle illusion:* A fine, close tulle. *Tunic dress:* Also tunic-robe; dress with tunic element (open medium-length jacket) or tunic effect, revealing much of the inner dress. *Velvet:* Silk fabric with thick, soft pile. *Zébrine:?* (a fabric).

1. "Neapolitan" hat, velvet cravat, waistcoat of
gros de Naples and redingote with collar and lapels
in one piece. [No. 704.]

2. Satin hat, velvet dress, embroidered crepe scarf.
[No. 706.]

3.   Outfit for a 3- to 5-year-old boy and "chevalière" for a 6- to 9-year-old boy. *[No. 708 (?).]*

4.   "Doña María" gauze beret, crepe dress with ribbon trim. *[No. 709.]*

5. Fashions for Longchamp. Rice-straw hat, dress of gros de Naples trimmed with openwork braid passementerie. *[No. 714.]*

6. Fashions for Longchamp. Hat of gros de Naples, embroidered laine foulard dress. *[No. 715.]*

7. Fashions for Longchamp. Rice-straw hat, dress of finely striped gros de Naples, embroidered tulle cuffs and mantilla. *[No. 716.]*

8. Fashions for Longchamp. Rice-straw hat with auricula-leaf trim, organdy canezou [jacket], printed muslin dress. *[No. 718.]*

9. Fashions for Longchamp. Crepe bonnet (capote) trimed with blonde, redingote [type of dress]
of gros de Naples. *[No. 720.]*

10. Fashions for Longchamp. Crepe hat, dress of
gros de Naples. *[No. 722.]*

11. Rice-straw bonnet, dress of gros de Naples,
embroidered tulle canezou. *[No. 723.]*

12. "Night green" redingote. *[No. 724.]*

13.   Crepe hat, cashmere dress with silk embroidery. *[No. 733.]*

14.   Satin hat with velvet lining, "gros d'Orient"
redingote [dress]. *[No. 768.]*

15.   Velvet beret, "satin royal" dress. *[No. 769.]*

16.   Crepe dress trimmed with ribbons and tulle, hairdo with garland. *[No. 770.]*

17.   Crepe-lisse dress with ribbon trim. *[No. 778.]*

18.   Satin dress with blonde appliqué. *[No. 779.]*

19. Velvet headdress, embroidered challis dress.
[No. 781.]

20. Crepe-illusion dress, satin pelerine, necklace of pearls and mother-of-pearl. [No. 782.]

21. Turban adorned with gems, gauze dress with ribbon trim. *[No. 789.]*

22. Riding habit with silk embroidery. *[No. 79?.]*

23. Headdress with plumes and gems, satin dress with feather trim, feather boa. *[No. 792.]*

24. Blonde beret, embroidered challis dress. *[No. 795.]*

25. Fashions for Longchamp. Dress of embroidered gros de Naples. *[No. 797.]*

26. Fashions for Longchamp. Diamond-pattern muslin dress, embroidered "bayadere" pelerine with fringe. *[No. 799.]*

27. Blonde cap, "paper-mulberry" [*mûrier de Chine*] dress, embroidered tulle mantilla. *[No. 806.]*

28. Indian muslin dress, rice-straw hat, printed cashmere shawl. *[No. 807.]*

29. Rice-straw hat, muslin dress, tulle canezou. *[No. 809.]*

30. Rice-straw hat, skirt of gros de Naples, embroidered muslin canezou. *[No. 810.]*

31. Rice-straw hat, dress of mousselaine de soie, embroidered tulle canezou. *[No. 814.]*

32. Rice-straw hat, embroidered muslin dress. *[No. 816.]*

33. Rice-straw hat, pinhead (pointillé) muslin dress, embroidered muslin canezou. *[No. 817; July 5, 1831.]*

34. Rice-straw hat, "Doña María" muslin dress. *[No. 818; July 10, 1831.]*

35. Hat of gros de Naples, challis morning dress
(peignoir). *[No. 819; July 15, 1831.]*

36. Rice-straw hat, organdy dress, needlepoint-
lace mantilla. *[No. 820; July 20, 1831.]*

37. Rice-straw hat, dress of mousselaine de soie, embroidered tulle canezou. *[No. 821; July 25, 1831.]*

38. Crepe hat, challis dress with seamless back, underskirt open at the side. *[No. 824; August 5, 1831.]*

39. Dress of mousselaine de soie, crepe hat.
[No. 827; August 20, 1831.]

40. Moire hat, embroidered tulle canezou. [No. 831;
September 5, 1831.]

41. Challis dress, moire hat. *[No. 832; September 10, 1831.]*

42. Rice-straw hat, jaconet dress, French cashmere shawl. *[No. 835; September 25, 1831.]*

43. Satin hat, moire redingote [dress], embroidered cashmere scarf. *[No. 838; October 5, 1831.]*

44. Crepe hat, embroidered challis redingote. *[No. 839; October 10, 1831.]*

45. Satin beret, embroidered merino dress.
[No. 840; October 15, 1831.]

46. Moire hat, satin dress with marten trim,
"Grand Lama" mantle. [No. 841; October 20, 1831.]

47. Moire hat, challis dress. *[No. 845; November 5, 1831.]*

48. Satin redingote [dress], satin and velvet hat with rooster feather, embroidered velvet muff. *[No. 846; November 10, 1831.]*

49.   Velvet hat, dress of "crêpe volant," blonde
sleeves and scarf. *[No. 847; November 15, 1831.]*

50.   Satin bibi [hat] trimmed with feathers, embroidered cashmerienne dress, marten boa and muff.
[No. 848; November 20, 1831.]

51. Moire dress, blonde mantilla and sleeves.
[No. 849; November 25, 1831.]

52. Casual wear. Redingote with woolen trim, coat with faceted and guilloched buttons, checked woolen trousers. *[No. 850; November 25, 1831.]*

53.   Velvet hat, dress of tulle Arachné. *[No. 851; November 30, 1831.]*

54.   "Etruscan" headdress with feathers and ears of grain, Esmeralda dress. *[No. 853; December 10, 1831.]*

55.   Velvet hat, embroidered challis redingote
[dress] and percale underskirt. *[No. 854; December 15, 1831.]*

56.   Ribbon headdress, blonde tunic dress, jet
jewelry. *[No. 861; January 15, 1832.]*

57. Crepe dress embroidered with chenille and gold, headdress with plume. *[No. 873; March 5, 1832.]*

58. Satin dress faced with velvet, satin and velvet hat. *[No. 874; March 10, 1832.]*

59. Ferronnière headdress, crepe dress, imitation-blonde pelerine, jet jewelry. *[No. 877; March 25, 1832.]*

60. Crepe dress with ribbon trim. *[No. 880; April 5, 1832.]*

61. Summer riding habit. Wool skirt, pleated batiste canezou, Italian straw hat (Leghorn). *[No. 881;
April 10, 1832.]*

62. Fashions for Longchamp. Crepe or moire hat,
redingote [dress] of "étoffe Chantilly," moire gaiters
with silk embroidery. *[No. 884; April 25, 1832.]*

63. Fashions for Longchamp. Rice-straw or Italian straw hat, dress of chiné gros de Naples. *[No. 887; May 5, 1832.]*

64. Fashions for Longchamp. Crepe hat, silk batiste dress. *[No. 888; May 10, 1832.]*

65. Hat of gros de Naples, dress of chiné gros de
Naples, embroidered muslin mantilla. *[No. 895; June
10, 1832.]*

66. Organdy dress, crepe hat trimmed with
flowers, embroidered tulle pelerine. *[No. 896; June
15, 1832.]*

67.   Rice-straw hat, dress of mousselaine de soie.
[No. 898, June 25, 1832.]

68.   Italian straw hat, embroidered tulle canezou,
dress of wool batiste, cashmere shawl; garden bench
of hollow iron. *[No. 900; June 30, 1832.]*

69. Foulard dress, Italian straw hat, embroidered
muslin pelerine. *[No. 916; September 10, 1832.]*

70. Rice-straw hat, moire redingote [dress] with or
without pelerine. *[No. 917; September 15, 1832.]*

71.   Embroidered or goffered tulle cap, jaconet morning dress (peignoir). *[No. 918; September 20, 1832.]*

72.   Dress of mousselaine de laine, hat of gros des Indes, embroidered tulle canezou. *[No. 919; September 25, 1832.]*

73. Hat of gros des Indes with velvet lining, red-ingote [dress] of embroidered [mousselaine?] Thibet. *[No. 931; November 15, 1832.]*

74. Lady's mantle and gentleman's redingote. *[No. 932; November 20, 1832.]*

75. Headdress trimmed with marabou (stork) feathers, blonde dress, foulard mantle. *[No. 935, November 20, 1832.]*

76. Satin hat, satin redingote [dress] with marten trim. *[No. 937; December 10, 1832.]*

77. Fashions for the theater. Lamé gauze turban, "Oriental" satin mantle lined with velvet, "satin royal" dress. *[No. 942; December 31, 1832.]*

78. Velvet hat, satin redingote [dress] faced with velvet, jet ornaments, blonde inner dress. *[No. 946; January 20, 1833.]*

79. Evening dress. *[No. 948; January 25, 1833.]*

80. Ribbon headdress, dress of embroidered gros de Naples, blonde mantilla. *[No. 952; February 15, 1833.]*

81. Turban, embroidered lamé tulle dress. *[No. 956; February 28, 1833.]*

82. Short cape of lace. *[No. 957; March 5, 1833.]*

83.   Plumed and jeweled headdress, blonde dress.
[No. 959; March 15, 1833.]

84.   Terry-velvet hat, embroidered pekin dress,
embroidered reversible crepe scarf. *[No. 961; March
25, 1833.]*

85. Wedding gown of silk brocade. *[No. 963;*
March 31, 1833.]

86. Fashions for Longchamp. Rice-straw hat, redingote [dress] of embroidered gros de Naples, filet
and cashmere scarf. *[No. 969; April 30, 1833.]*

87.   Fashions for Longchamp. "Doña María" gauze hat, redingote [dress] of "zébrine." *[No. 971; May 5, 1833.]*

88.   Fashions for Longchamp. Openwork straw "Greek" bonnet, muslin dress, embroidered tulle pelerine. *[No. 972; May 10, 1833.]*

89.   Rice-straw hat, dress of embroidered poult de soie. [No. 973; May 15, 1833.]

90.   Crepe hat, redingote [dress] of gros de Naples trimmed with black lace. [No. 976; May 30, 1833.]

91. Rice-straw hat, embroidered organdy dress.
[No. 978; June 5, 1833.]

92. Blonde and ribbon headdress, dress of gros de Naples trimmed with lace, filet mittens. *[No. 979; June 10, 1833.]*

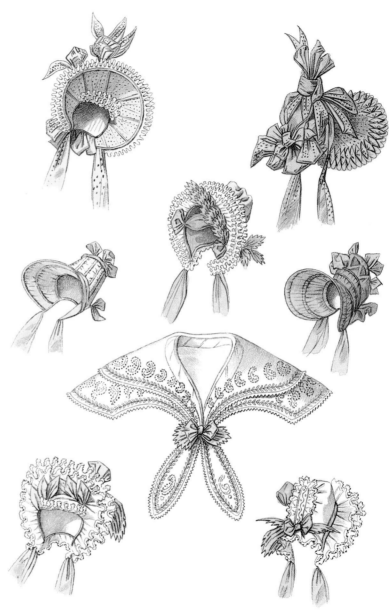

93. Italian straw hat, dress of chiné gros de Naples.
[No. 980; June 15, 1833.]

94. (1): Ribboned bonnet. (2): Muslin bonnet. (3) Muslin canezou. (4 & 5): Girls' hats. (6): Tulle cap.
[No. 121/980; June 15, 1833.]

95.   Crepe hat, blonde mantilla, gauze batiste dress.
[No. 981; June 20, 1833.]

96.   Hat of gros de Naples with hem, embroidered
and lined muslin redingote [dress]. [No. 982; June
25, 1833.]

97.   Rice-straw hat, dress of chiné gros de Naples
with designs "en diminutif." *[No. 985; July 5, 1833.]*

98.   Hat of "tissu de l'Inde" trimmed with roses,
morning dress (peignoir) of embroidered
mousselaine de laine. *[No. 987; July 15, 1833.]*

99. Sewn straw hat, redingote [dress] of
mousselaine de soie with ribbon trim. [No. 997;
August 30, 1833.]

100. Organdy dress. [No. 999; September 5, 1833.]

101. Blonde cap, embroidered organdy dress. *[No. 1001; September 15, 1833.]*

102. Dress of "satin à volonté," dress of satin blonde. *[No. 1003; September 25, 1833.]*

103.   Satin hat, lace veil, broché dress. *[No. 1009; October 20, 1833.]*

104.   Turban, mantles of "Ali Baba" cloth and "Braganza" cloth. *[No. 1010; October 25, 1833.]*

105.   Crepe hat, satin dress. *[No. 1011; October 31, 1833.]*

106.   Sleeved capes trimmed with astrakhan (karakul, Persian lamb). *[No. 1012; October 31, 1833.]*

107. Gauze turban trimmed with argus-pheasant feathers, tunic dress of "foulard de Smyrne," embroidered-crepe inner dress. *[No. 1024; December 20, 1833.]*

108. Embroidered tulle dress, satin bodice trim. *[No. 1025; December 25, 1833.]*

109.   Figured gauze dress with ribbon trim. *[No. 1028; January 5, 1834.]*

110.   Velvet "Gothic" hat, velvet dress. *[No. 1029; January 10, 1834.]*

111. Hairdo with plumes and diamonds, gauze outer dress, satin inner dress. *[No. 1042; February 28, 1834.]*

112. Headdress with "grape gauze" [gauze grapes?], tulle-illusion outer dress, satin inner dress. *[No. 1044; March 5, 1834.]*

113.   Crepe turban trimmed with "chefes" [??] and gold fringe, gold lamé tulle dress. *[No. 1045; March 10, 1834.]*

114.   Cap trimmed with marabou (stork) feathers, dress of gros de Naples trimmed with crepe ruching and satin ribbons. *[No. 1046; March 15, 1834.]*

115. Wedding gown of embroidered muslin, "Cimodocée" [Cymodoce, a Greek sea nymph] hair styling. *[No. 1048; March 20, 1834.]*

116. Hat of "satin armure," "Haïdée" [heroine of Byron's *Don Juan*] satin dress, embroidered satin mantilla. *[No. 1105; October 31, 1834.]*

117.   Figured-satin turban, ermine mantle. *[No. 1107; November 5, 1834.]*

118.   Velvet and gauze turban, gold-embroidered satin gown for presentation at court. *[No. 1111; November 20, 1834.]*

119.   Gauze dress with satin bodice trim. *[No. 1115;*
December 5, 1834.]

120.   Embroidered-crepe dress with blonde trim.
[No. 1116; December 10, 1834.]